LITTLE KOALA

Holt, Rinehart and Winston
New York

LITTLE KOALA

by Suzanne Noguere
and Tony Chen

illustrated by Tony Chen

Text copyright © *1979 by Suzanne Noguere and Tony Chen*
Illustrations copyright © *1979 by Tony Chen*
All rights reserved, including the right to reproduce
this book or portions thereof in any form.
Published simultaneously in Canada by Holt, Rinehart
and Winston of Canada, Limited.
Printed in the United States of America
10 9 8 7 6 5 4 3 2 1

Library of Congress Cataloging in Publication Data

Noguere, Suzanne.   Little Koala.

   SUMMARY: Follows a little koala in Australia
from its birth to separation from its mother
when a year old.
   1. Koalas—Juvenile literature. [1. Koalas]
I. Chen, Tony, joint author. II. Title.
QL737.M38N63   599′.2   78-17112
ISBN 0-03-044041-6

To Ira Silberlicht—S. N.

To Pura—T. C.

LITTLE KOALA

It is daytime in a forest in Australia. The koala is dozing in her eucalyptus tree. The wombat in his burrow and the brushtailed possum in a hole at the base of the tree are asleep. Only the powerful owl, the tawny frogmouth bird, and the sugar glider happen to be awake.

A baby koala has just been born. But no one sees it. Not even its mother.

No wonder! The baby that has left her womb is a pink speck, no bigger than a fly. Blind and deaf, it smells her pouch and climbs toward it. If the baby gets lost in the fur, it will die. The mother might even brush it off accidentally.

But this baby arrives. It slips into its mother's pouch and drinks milk from her nipple there. No one in the forest has seen it. Only the mother knows it has been born. She can feel it suckling. The baby will keep growing in the pouch.

At nightfall the animals wake up. The mother koala yawns. Everyone is hungry.

The animals hunt for food. The brush-tailed possum chooses a small bird; the sugar glider catches insects; the tawny frogmouth captures a mouse.

The mother koala does not eat other animals. And she does not have to hunt. Her food is on the eucalyptus tree.

All night long she eats the leaves of the tree in which she sleeps all day. And she never has to climb down the tree to get water. She gets all the moisture she needs from the leaves. That's why the people of Australia call her koala. It means "the animal that never drinks."

The mother koala wants to move to a tree with more leaves. She walks out on a high branch until it tips over and touches the next tree. She has made a bridge to walk across. Now she has a new supply of leaves. She picks her leaves carefully. Some are good to eat but some are poisonous. She can tell the difference by smelling them.

Half a year goes by and still no one has seen her baby. One night, the baby peeks out of its mother's pouch. What a busy world it sees! It jumps out and looks around. Everyone in the forest gazes at it in surprise.

Soon, the baby is a familiar sight in the forest.

The powerful owl has been staring at the little koala for some time. Strong as the owl is, he cannot carry off a grown koala. But he might snatch a young one.

Rising on great wings, he flies through
the forest. Frightened little koala drops
the leaf it is eating and jumps into safety
— mother's pouch. The powerful owl is
forced to hunt for food elsewhere.

Before long, little koala is too big to enter its mother's pouch. It rides on her back wherever she goes.

When there are no more leaves on their tree, they look for another tree. The mother moves slowly across the forest floor. Suddenly, she begins to run. She has seen her enemy, a wild dog called the dingo.

The dingo bares his teeth and barks. He wants to kill the little koala for dinner.

Although the mother has sharp claws, she is no match for this savage hunter. She leaps up a tree and jumps higher and higher up, until she and her baby are safe.

The baby grows bigger each day. One year after birth, it is almost as large as its mother. And it is still riding piggyback! Little koala loves it. But the mother finds that the baby is getting too heavy.

One day, when little koala climbs on its mother's back, she pushes it away. Little koala is shocked. Its feelings are hurt. It tries again. Again she pushes it away.

Little koala begins to cry. The forest fills with the sound of sobbing.

For a while, little koala stays in the same tree, as close to its mother as it can without making her angry. As the days go by, it gets used to being apart from her.

Little koala decides to try the leaves of another eucalyptus tree. It walks out almost to the edge of a branch but does not jump. The tree is too far away. It would be dangerous to jump.

Slowly, little koala climbs down to a lower branch. It sits awhile, measuring the distance, then leaps. Crash! It lands on a branch of the new tree. Its grip is strong and it holds on safely.

Little koala explores the
new eucalyptus tree.
It picks a spot that looks
comfortable. It grooms itself,
using the toes of its hindfoot
as a comb, then falls asleep.

Little koala has a tree of
its own now. When night falls,
it will wake up and taste
the leaves of its new tree.

About the Authors

Suzanne Noguere, a native New Yorker and graduate of Barnard College, is a poet whose work has appeared in *The Nation, Poetry, Jazz,* and *Heresies*. A mutual appreciation of animals led the author and artist to collaborate on this work.

Tony Chen, a former art director for *Newsweek* magazine, is also a painter and sculptor. Many of his paintings, watercolors, and pieces of sculpture are in private collections.

A cum laude graduate of Pratt Institute, he has illustrated a number of children's books, among them *Too Many Crackers, About Owls,* and *It's About Birds*. He lives with his wife and two sons on Long Island.